A Beginner's Guide to Archangels

The Magick of Archangels: the Power of the Divine

Conrad Bauer

Disclaimer

Contents

Disclaimer..3

Contents 5

Introduction..1

History of archangels 3

Modern interpretations 7

Roles and capabilities of Archangels 13

First-hand accounts of Archangels 23

Who are the archangels? 57

    Michael 57

    Raphael 59

    Gabriel 61

    Uriel 63

    Chamuel..65

    Jophiel 66

    Raguel 67

    Other Archangels 69

        Ariel 69

        Azrael...70

        Camael..71

        Haniel 71

        Jeremiel/Ramiel 72

        Metatron...73

        Raziel 75

        Sandalphon...76

Finding your archangel 79

    Using astrology 79

    Using Numerology...81

How to invoke Archangels 85

Invocation for fulfilment 85

Prayer for Protection..87

A protection for travelers 90

An invocation for achieving goals 91

A call to dreams 93

Conclusion 97

Further reading..99

About the Author..101

Introduction

Have you ever felt there might be a presence watching over you? Have you ever tried to reach beyond the veil of typical human comprehension in an effort to understand the supernatural? For those who are fascinated by a world beyond our own or those who have ever felt alone in the universe, it can be reassuring to think that there might be someone or something watching over you. For many people, these silent watchers are the archangels.

Over many centuries and across many cultures, people have often recognized the existence of archangels. In various societies, they have often received different names. With a similar function and role across the world, they are often protective spirits. They reach out to us mere mortals and offer protection, guidance, reassurance, and the hope that there might be something more to life that just what we see in the world around us. In these instances, the existence of archangels is a fiercely personal and essential phenomena.

But how can you move yourself closer to the world of the archangels? While some people find comfort in conventional religion, the modern interpretation of angels can often offer us the chance to become involved with the Divine in a truly different way. Over the course of the last centuries, we have developed and refined our knowledge and understanding of the archangels. This has culminated in what we know today. For anyone who is interested in bolstering their relationship with their archangel, this book will aim to offer real insight.

Not only will we look at the history of archangels, but we will be able to delve deeper into how exactly they can be summoned and how they can play a role in your life. If you have ever wondered about exactly how you can form a relationship with your archangel, this is the book for you. Read on to discover more about the magick of the archangels.

History of archangels

In order to understand the phenomena of archangels, it can help to have an understanding of what the word, the phrase, and the ideas have come to represent over the past centuries. In western society, many people's interpretation of archangels and angels in general comes from the Christian tradition. This could be as simple as the image of cherubic babies with wings, sitting on clouds and playing harps. It could be the beings that serve under God and do his bidding in the world. It can even take on abstract and complicated ideas that defy typical real-world expectations. But to consider the Christian interpretation (and to better understand modern archangels), we also need to consider the role of angels in all of the Abrahamic religions. As intertwined as they are, Islam, Judaism, and Christianity all present a version of the angelic ranks to the world. But what do we need to know about the history of religious archangels?

Etymologically speaking, the word archangel comes from Greek. The first part of the word, "arch," can be roughly translated as "chief," indicating the status these particular angels have when compared to other angelic figures. While many people might be familiar with the concept of angels, the idea of archangels can be viewed as an entirely different entity.

Across the three major Abrahamic religions, the two most prominent of the archangels are traditionally Michael and Gabriel. Referred to throughout many of the books that make up the Bible, the Quran, and the Torah, these figures are sometimes joined by Raphael. As you pour through the history of the various branches of Christianity, however, it emerges that there are differences of opinion on whether Raphael should join Michael and Gabriel in these exalted ranks. Islam also mentions Azrael and Israfil, while Judaism refers to Metatron as being an archangel.

Over the course of religious history, the idea of the archangels is markedly different from our contemporary interpretations. One of the more commonly held views includes a pantheon of seven archangels commonly held to be the most important. As well as the aforementioned Gabriel, Michael, and Raphael, many earlier religious scholars also included Uriel, Raguel, Remiel, and Saraqael. These figures (or at the very least, texts that mention them) are referred to in the Bible and can trace their lineage back to the early church workers who helped develop many of the core tenants of Christianity. Pope Gregory I, later made a Saint, leaves one of the first written clues of the seven archangels and makes a point of listing those angels whom he believes should be included in the category of archangels.

In knowing how the pantheon of archangels has changed, we can notice that the names of those included are rarely fixed. With so many different cultures and societies unable to agree on even the identity of as many as seven archangels, it has taken centuries for our knowledge to become more coalesced. Some people might find it strange that the modern interpretation of archangels can stray so far from the traditional narrative. Thankfully, in examining the history of the beings, we can notice that they are not fixed. There is no correct or incorrect version of the history of archangels. In dealing with such spiritual beings, the potential for interpretation and personal reflection is massive. While it can help to have a broad overview of the differing historical patterns of archangels, we can also observe that there is no one correct answer. As you will notice during this book, the ability to harness the power of the archangels for yourself depends very little on the words written in the Torah or the Quran. Instead, the very fact that some of the world's most powerful and widely followed religions each hold the concept so close to their beliefs should be seen as a reflection of an inherent truth and quality in the phenomena of the archangels.

Modern interpretations

Even though the idea of archangels and their power has been around for many millennia, it is only now that we are beginning to harness and interpret their abilities in different manners. Legends tell of magickal practitioners who could summon the spirits and archangels during the time before Christ was born. From the various shaman found around the world to the priests who worked in temples using Solomon's keys, many people have claimed to have been able to call on archangels to do their bidding or offer them help. While these secrets were previously guarded as sacred knowledge, tireless work by modern researchers has opened up the possibility of being able to summon archangels without having to spend your life as a priest or magickal researcher.

Instead, modern views of archangels are somewhat different. Today, it is typically held that archangels are beings who are capable of extraordinary power. As extensions of a greater divine presence, they are able to capture a small amount of the grace held by a higher being. In representing such a vital and important power, they can come in many forms. One of their greatest abilities is to heal. As healers, they can take on many forms. They can conduct surgery on our broken bodies or heal the emotional tears that can rip through a soul. With the power of the Divine, they can hold life and death in their hands. Arriving on Earth in metaphysical forms, it can be difficult to reach out and touch them. Knowing that they walk among us, however, can be hugely reassuring.

For those who have read the Bible or other religious texts, the notion of the Divine will be familiar. Regardless of your own personal opinions on the existence of God or the particular nature of such a being, the archangels represent just a tiny slice of such a power. If we are to consider a divine creator to be an all-powerful, omnipotent being, then those who do his bidding with only a small fraction of such a power are still many, many more times more capable than mere humans. It is this power to heal and to mend which gives archangels their true influence.

The way we interact with the archangels might differ from person to person. Some people choose to invoke their spirits daily, as part of a regular routine, while others pick and choose their moments to call in the divine healers. It might be that people turn to archangels when they find themselves in trouble, or that they simply use the protective qualities of the angels' power to guard them against future harm. There is no right or wrong way to choose to interact with the archangels. Though some methods and practices can be seen as more effective than others, the main tenant of a modern belief in their existence is faith. As ever in matters of faith, the actual details of the rituals themselves are not as important as the strength and honesty of the faith being used to back up the interaction. When dealing with modern interpretations of archangels, we often find that those with the strongest faith are those who see the best results.

So how do we feel the presence of archangels in our lives? For the majority of people, even the strongest of interactions will not be obvious. In the case of most of the public, the lack of awareness or even an unwillingness to stretch out comprehension beyond the physical plane can hinder the chance of witnessing real magick in day-to-day life. Should an archangel choose to interact with such people, these people can often come through the episode with no awareness of what actually occurred. Should they have been healed or otherwise benefitted from the angel's benevolence, they might put down their experiences to luck, chance, or simply not register a second thought. For the angel, this matters not. For those who are trying to invoke the protection of angels, this can seem almost unfair. But the goodness and the divinity of the archangels is capable of touching every person. When learning the arts contained within this book, we will find that the modern interpretation of the archangels does not provide any element of control over these divine beings.

Instead, it can open up a relationship with their power. By doing as much as possible to strengthen the bond between yourself and the archangels, you can discover just how much more powerful, rich, and rewarding life can be when invoking the power of said beings. While we might not be able to control such powerful beings, we can build a bond with them that raises our chances of comprehending the Divine. As well as improving your physical and mental life, a well-formed and comprehensive knowledge of the world of the archangels can be vital to your spiritual well-being.

For modern believers in the world of the archangels, their existence is less a debated piece of Christian, Jewish, or Islamic theology. Instead, it is a means of expanding knowledge of the Divine. It is a form of spirituality. By learning the processes, incantations, and invocations contained later in this book, you should find that your understanding of the metaphysical and the phenomenal strengthens as you become better acquainted with the ideas we will explore. For those who are seeking power and the ability to control, modern archangel lore does not cater for you. Instead, a belief in archangels in the modern world can bring self-improvement, life satisfaction, protection, and healing into your world. As much about improving one's self as it is about learning the particular nature of the spiritual, it is not uncommon for those involved in the modern world of the archangel interpretation to find themselves happier and more at ease with themselves once they have expanded their knowledge.

Now that you have a better understanding of what archangels and their place in modern society do, we can move on to getting to know the archangels and how they will relate to you as an individual.

Roles and capabilities of Archangels

In picking up this guide to archangels, you will probably have a vague idea of the potential power and ability of divine beings. But the truth is that few people truly comprehend the actual capabilities of the archangels. In reading through this book thus far, we have given a broad idea of the historical and modern conception of the archangels, but we have hardly touched on how they interact with and appear in day-to-day life. If you are at all interested in involving yourself in the world of the archangels, then this will not only be one of the most important chapters, but also one of the most complex. In the coming pages, we will discuss how the archangels are able to alter, change, influence, and improve your life.

Perhaps the most important aspect of learning about archangels is knowing how incredibly different they are from humanity. The majority of people are so firmly rooted in their conception of daily human life that they are simply unable to comprehend the manner in which an angel might exist. While they are able to envisage, sympathize with, and empathize with family members, friends, or even strangers, trying to relate in the same fashion to an angelic being is simply not possible. Due to their very nature, being able to understand what it means to be an archangel is vastly different to being able to relate to your fellow human being.

But why is this the case? Well, put simply, the divine nature of the archangels separates their nature from our own. While we might share similar properties with the archangels, since we are both creations of a higher power, we are not the same. As anyone who has spent any time reading Christian or other Abrahamic doctrine will know, the legions of angels do not fulfil a purpose like that of humanity. Rather than existing on Earth, they transcend many planes. Rather than having to deal in matters of faith and belief, their closeness to God is pre-arranged. Their ability to realize and wield this power while traversing between heaven and the mortal plane grants them power beyond anything we might be able to comprehend. And therein lies the problem. So different is the world of the archangel that the layman simply cannot see into their mindset without the correct training and a willingness to stretch faith into the world of the paranormal.

This is the first hurdle that many people try to encounter when approaching the subject of archangels. But in the cases of those who wish to develop and further their understanding of this divine and unknown plane, the very act of opening this book is a demonstration of the willingness and drive required in order to bring the power of the angels into your life. If we are to accept that angels and archangels are a legitimate force in this world (and in reading this far into the book, this can be taken as a given), then we can begin to map out and understand exactly how they influence our lives on an everyday basis.

As we have mentioned previously in the book, one of the key roles archangels play in the world is as healers. The healing nature of angelic power is essential, and it is one of their defining characteristics. For much of the history of organized religion, we have seen angels as a key link between humanity and the Divine. They help with communication and assist with humanity's comprehension of the Creator. In this regard, their history as healers is more than simply medical. Instead, they have been healing the relationship between man and God. Their healing properties are vital to the history of man, repairing, guiding, and nurturing a key element of human kindness, divinity, and belief. As healers, the pantheon of archangels are able to improve our philosophical, religious, metaphysical, and soulful malaises with the same skill that they might use to treat a wound or a broken bone. In this respect, their healing power is a many sided shape; one essential quality (healing) that is demonstrated in a variety of fashions.

This is one of the most difficult things to comprehend about the role of angels. Though their key responsibility is to heal, this manifests itself in a myriad of ways. They might be bringing peace to the distraught or delivering compassion to those in need. They might be guiding the lost and the unaware. Their roles are often abstract and obscure, but at their heart lies a determination to help heal the world. And this is where we come in. In making yourself aware of the power of the archangels, you can invoke their qualities in order to bring a healing glow into your life. This can help you overcome challenges, solve problems, and resolve tricky situations.

Not only are their powers reactionary, but those best versed in the discourse of the archangels can find themselves preemptively invoking the Divine beings in order to better protect themselves against challenges that lie ahead. If you are worried about a specific upcoming event that might compromise or harm you, then being able to bring about the protective, healing qualities of the archangels in advance can be incredibly useful. Not only are they able to protect you from harm, but they can act as a guiding force and help you navigate even the most tricky periods.

In offering their healing abilities to the world, there are few things which are required of people in return. As ever with matters of faith, one of the key issues is always belief. Those who find themselves achieving the best results when following the advice laid out in this book are often those whose faith is the strongest. Those who are able to give themselves wholeheartedly to the world of the archangels will foster and develop a stronger bond quicker than those who are more skeptical. As ever with beginner guides, however, you might find yourself struggling at first. Despite this, it is more important than ever to never drop your faith in the roles and the capabilities of the legion of archangels and their healing powers.

During this chapter, we have chiefly dealt in the abstract. This makes it a very difficult chapter to get through. The roles of the archangels and their attendant capabilities are very rooted in the idea of healing. However, due to the multiple ways in which this property manifests, being able to point to real-world, physical results is difficult. Already existing across a multitude of planes of existence, some people find it hard to pinpoint a place in the world in which archangels could legitimately function. In choosing to read their existence as they might an exotic animal or culture, they wish to find actual evidence of angels being present. Empirical evidence is tough to come by, however. Being touched by the healing powers of an angel very rarely leaves a mark. It very rarely leaves so much as a memory. Instead, it can often touch directly onto the soul, imprinting their presence on the human condition itself. Due to the metaphysical nature of this practice, certain people find themselves dismissing the idea.

However, those who deny the existence of archangels are not exempt from their healing benefits. It might seem strange to some people that refusing to belief in the Divine qualities of these beings should not drive them away. But that is not their role in the world. As creatures of God, they strive to further the teachings of the Divine and bring a touch of religion to even the nonreligious. In this respect, even those who have forthrightly denied the existence of angels can be visited by a healing spirit. While those of us who work to understand the relationship between humanity and the spiritual might be able to form better bonds with angels and their like, the agnostics of the world are not excluded. Instead, the warm, glowing touch of the archangels can still reach into their lives and heal their bodies and spirit.

So, with this in mind, what are the roles and the capabilities of the archangels? How do they affect our lives? How can we know when we've been touched by their presence? How can we know that we have felt their existence in our souls?

This is, again, hard to quantify. For those who have never interacted with the angelic beings, describing such an encounter often sounds like gibberish. Those who talk of such meetings often describe a warmth, a general feeling of reassurance. Regardless of the context in which they encountered the angel, they can tell of a specific feeling of assured well-being, as though everything suddenly became right in the world. It can be almost like scratching at an itch or standing in the sun on a hot day. Rather than a specific physical feeling, it is more often than not felt in the bones and deep within the body. Everyone who has told a tale of their close encounter with an archangel will bring up the pleasant feeling of contentment that derived from the moment the angel arrived.

As messengers and subjects of God, it is often the role and the responsibility of the archangels to bring a tiny slither of the Divine blessing into the world. With the power to heal, this blessing is a communication from the greater beings and is beyond the scope of human convention. While we may not be able to look on the face of God himself, we can experience a small fraction of his power in our interactions with angels. As such, they can bring faith and wonder into the world. For humans, these encounters might even pass by unnoticed. Not everyone is capable of noticing the blessing that enters into their life. They can, however, sense the tremendous feeling of well-being that results from these moments. Whether they choose to ascribe this pleasantness and this healing to archangels or some other phenomena does not matter. In bringing a little extra good into the world, the archangels are furthering God's will.

We have talked at length about the healing qualities of the archangels. When discussing their capabilities, this often means that we will have to acknowledge that they are not placed on Earth to perform life shattering changes. Unlike Jesus or prophets, their power and influence is more understated. Although they are able to heal, repair, and mend, they are not able to create. While this takes on many forms and offers a great deal of protection to those who know how to wield the power, it is very important that we remember that the abilities of the archangels are not something that is there to be used by humanity as a tool or weapon. Anyone who wishes to welcome archangels into their life must do so with good intentions. The limitations of the powers of the archangels are often moral. Those using the powers for narcissistic or selfish reasons will often find they achieve little. Those who are trying to undermine, harm, or damage another will never prosper. This is simply not within the capabilities of beings such as archangels.

What they are capable of, however, is often much more powerful. As anyone with faith will be able to explain, the opportunity to power this belief into a righteous cause can beget amazing results. When combined with the inherent healing capabilities of the archangels, there is little that is not possible for those with the correct knowledge. Whether you're praying for help for a sick relative or simply asking for protection during a time you know will be tough, those with good intentions, a belief in the power of the Divine, and the knowledge of archangels can achieve amazing results. As we will discover later in this book, there are specific incantations and invocations designed to achieve specific results. But to this point, we have dealt too long in the work of the philosophical and the abstract. Before we go any further, it can help to learn about a number of real life examples of people who have welcomed archangels into their lives.

First-hand accounts of Archangels

One of the best ways in which we can discover more about the nature of archangels is by reading the accounts of those who have interacted with them in the past. Through these encounters, we can witness the truth behind the capabilities of these beings and discover a little more about how they can affect our lives. From those who have actively sought out their guardians to those who have been converted to the cause after being randomly blessed, these accounts give us context and depth when thinking about how archangels might be able to change our lives.

Over the course of the coming pages, you will be able to read a number of true stories about those who have experienced firsthand the touch of an archangel. These stories come in many varieties, "angel-medium." For the uninitiated, this is someone who believes they have the power to act as a conduit for the archangels. Through a combination of practice and faith, they have gained the power to channel the abilities and healing processes of the Divine beings. As someone who is truly enamored by the phenomenon, it makes an excellent starting point for the discussion.

The first person's name is Sarah. Her encounter tells of receiving a message from an archangel named Michael. At the time, she believes that Michael was spreading his influence across the world and those who believed in his powers were better placed to receive his blessing. His love and his desire to help came to Sarah when she needed it most. Despite being one of the highest ranking and busiest archangels, her encounter with Michael shows the reach that the angels have when entering into our world.

As an angel medium, Sarah works closely with the Divine spirits on a daily basis. In doing so, she can observe firsthand the way in which they influence the world. Despite this proximity to the angels' power, she confesses that she was astonished to see the effect that Michael could have on her life when she reached out to him. Among the things that impressed her most was the superhuman speed with which the angels could react. This speed, Sarah suggests, shows the extent to which the angels really do care.

The story itself takes place in January of 1998. During this time, Archangel Michael influenced Sarah's life in an incredibly positive way. On the night in question, the rain was falling. The storm was heavy and the visibility on the road was incredibly poor. It was hard to see far in any direction. Regardless, Sarah and her friends had decided that they were going to dinner. For weeks, they had planned to visit an Indian restaurant. Something as simple as a storm was not going to stop them. The restaurant itself was right next to an old railway track, which was in turn near the docking station for ferries that had since shut down. In order to reach the restaurant, Sarah and her friends were required to cross over the railway tracks and get to the parking lot on the other side. When they tried to get across, however, the car got stuck. Trying to pull forward and backwards, Sarah and her three friends realized that they were going nowhere. The car could not move.

Trying to find out what the problem was, Sarah got out of the car. Despite the rain, she could see that the problem was more severe than she had previously thought. The car was firmly stuck on the tracks, and there seemed no way of shifting it. One of the wheels was raised off the ground and whenever the accelerator was pressed, it would just spin. Together, Sarah and her friends tried pushing the car. It didn't work. Instead, the car just became more and more stuck on the tracks. Perhaps the worst problem of all, however, was the fact that Sarah knew the train tracks to still be very much in use. With the storm hindering all visibility, the chances that a train engineer might be able to spot the car in the distance and slow down in time were close to zero. Sarah had no idea when the next train might arrive and neither of the two people had any idea how they might free the car. It was absolutely stuck in place.

Despite the four people being present, moving the car from the tracks seemed impossible. Without any mobile phone technology (it being 1998,) Sarah and one friend decided that they would walk to the restaurant anyway. Once there, they could call through to help and try and shift the car before a train arrived. With luck, they might still be able to make it in time to eat. They left behind the two others, who would try to think about any other way of moving the stuck vehicle.

Sarah and her friend reached the restaurant and called through to a tow truck. Sarah thought that though tow truck drivers usually helped with break downs and accidents, they also might be able to offer advice on the situation. While getting through on the restaurant's phone, however, they could only talk to a recording. With all of the representatives busy, Sarah was forced to wait in line to talk to someone. With the possibility of a train arriving at any time, waiting in a queue over the phone seemed like an awful idea. Sarah handed over the phone to her friend and asked her to wait on the line. Should the queue ever shorten and the call get through, the friend would be able to explain the situation and try to quickly get a tow truck out to help them. At this time, Sarah herself was beginning to have a better idea.

Up until this moment, the panic and the worry of the situation had taken over Sarah's mind. It had stopped her from thinking clearly. As an angel medium, there was only really one place she should have turned. She began to think about Michael and the healing powers he might be able to bring to the situation. Sarah decided that she would ask for help. Without having much time for invocations or the procedures she had come to know and love, Sarah simply reached out with the power of her mind. In a desperate situation, she asked Archangel Michael – wherever he was – to come and help her.

Sarah stepped out from the restaurant into the pouring rain. Despite the weather, she did not feel cold. After just two steps, she could feel a deep warmth within her. As she began to get closer and closer to the car, with the tracks becoming more and more visible, Sarah squinted into the distance. She could see movement around the car. Even before she could make out the full shape of the vehicle and see everything clearly, the feeling of warmth inside her grew and grew. And then, as suddenly as it had arrived, it went away. Standing in the rain, Sarah could finally see into the distance. There, the car was off the tracks and was driving towards her. It circled around the tracks, drove past Sarah into the car park, and found a space.

Afterwards, Sarah tried to figure out exactly what had happened. While she and the friend had stepped into the restaurant, the two other people had stayed behind to see if anything could be done. Out of nowhere, another person had come forward. It was one of the workers from the seemingly empty docks. The person had come across the stopped car and had offered to help. As a veteran of the docks, the worker knew instantly how the car had come to be stuck and advised the men of what exactly they needed to do in order to get out of the predicament. With the worker's advice put to good use, the car was moved from its stuck position, and after a little work, was finally free. The worker's appearance from nowhere was a surprise to everyone involved, with him seemingly having arrived just as Sarah had failed to get through with her phone call. When she thought about it afterwards, Sarah surmised that the worker had arrived almost the instant she had thought to ask for him. For her, the worker's appearance was none other than the angelic influence of Michael.

Following the freeing of the car, Sarah and her friends went into the restaurant and had their planned dinner.

After a brief thought, they ventured back out into the rain, thinking to ask the ferry worker to come and eat with them as a way of saying thanks. Looking around in the rain, however, it quickly became clear that the worker had already left, vanishing as quickly as he had arrived. This only cemented the worker's angelic qualities in the eyes of Sarah. When she thought about it afterwards, it was clear that the worker was operating under the influence and guiding hand of her healing angel, Michael.

If there was any doubt at all about the influence Michael had had on the situation, then Sarah was to have her suspicions reaffirmed later than evening. After the meal, the group sat at the table while the storm continued to rage through the night. Just as she checked out through the window to see the weather, Sarah caught a huge flash of lightning as it spread across the sky. This lightning bolt was special. Rather than the standard white color, it was a deep shade of blue. Sarah knew this to be the color most commonly associated with her chosen archangel, Michael. But that was not all. Rather than the standard fork shape that lightning takes when travelling to the ground, this bolt was shaped exactly like a sword, the very same weapon that depictions of Archangel Michael always show. For Sarah, this was simply her guardian angel confirming the fact that he had reached down and helped her when she had asked, when she was most in need.

After that night, Sarah's doubts about archangels and their powers were forever put to bed. Now, her position as an angel medium is bolstered by her powerful interactions with the capabilities of archangels. While she had known of their power before, these days, Sarah is utterly imbued with the belief in their potential. For Sarah, the events of that fateful night have confirmed to her what she already suspected: that the archangels remain a powerful and dependable source for good in the world, whose influence can be seen in even the most unlikely places.

Our next entry will detail more than a single incident. While Sarah had her faith confirmed, there are others who notice the angelic influence on their life over a long period of time. For some, this not only comes as a personal revelation, but inspires them to reach out to others. Just as this book is being written to help welcome others to the world of the archangel, certain authors have written down their thoughts and experiences to better help others understand the complicated relationship we humans experience with the Divine.

This next passage will deal with the experiences of a woman we will call Jane. Jane has written an entire book detailing her experiences with angels throughout her life. We will look into one chapter and note the lessons we can take from the situation. While some people might be reluctant to share such experiences, Jane is more than happy to let others know about how angel therapy played a big part in her life. Again, the archangel in question is none other than Michael.

When asked about the role Michael played in her life, Jane confirms that his role is one of guidance and protection. Through the relationship she shares with such a being, Jane is able to trust and call upon Michael during the most difficult times. She has even seen signs from him to reaffirm her faith when she had doubted him in the past.

These signs are important for Jane. She sees herself as someone who is reluctant to truly dedicate her life to one particular belief and admits that she has previously held doubts about the existence of such beings. During the moments when the signs appear, they are not as obvious as word written in the sky or a shape appearing in her coffee. Instead, they arrive like feelings in the pit of her stomach. These deep sensations occur just when Michael is crossing her mind. Alternatively, she has spotted more physical notices that the archangel is reaching out into the world around her, including one in which a feather floats down in such a way as to touch upon the one part of Jane's body that is experiencing pain, healing the area with its touch. As well as this, the noticing of the name Michael in certain meaningful places during her daily life helps Jane remain aware that the angel is always near and able to help.

During the course of the chapter in her book, Jane recalls the first time she heard about the existence and power of the archangels and felt compelled to try out it out herself. Despite believing in angels beforehand, she was skeptical of the influence they would be able to have in her life. As she delved deeper and deeper into the world of archangels, some of the things she read started to make sense. One of the phenomena she noticed most was the existence of things which arrived in threes. These might be numbers or letters grouped together or simply sounds that were repeated three times. Each time things like these occurred, Jane began to notice the influence of the angels around her.

One night, she mentions, she was beginning to drift into sleep. Almost falling into unconsciousness, she remembers asking the Archangel Michael to look after her. She did not use any of the traditional invocations.

She merely took advantage of her growing faith and spread the word out into the world. Just before dozing off, she remembers asking for protection from harm and a physical notification that the angel had entered into her life. Then she promptly fell asleep and almost forgot about everything.

Unlike most nights, Jane woke up before dawn. Still dark outside, she remembers feeling incredibly thirsty. This was most uncommon. Unperturbed, Jane stepped out of bed and walked down the hallway to fetch a glass of water. Arriving back at her bed, she discovered that she was unable to fall asleep once again. After failing to fall asleep, Jane decided to get up once more and stand by the window. She was captured by a sudden desire to look out into the world, rather than fruitlessly leave her head lying against a pillow.

Rising, Jane walked to the window and pulled back the curtain. Not uncommonly for the winter months, it was snowing outside. This was February, and it was likely to be the last time that year when the snow would fall in Jane's country. Jane loved the snow – it was one of her favorite things about the winter – but this weather was nowhere near enough to convince her that a prayer had been answered. Indeed, she had almost forgotten about the pleas she had sent out to Michael before falling asleep. Still early in the morning, Jane decided to check the time. She reached out for her phone and looked down at the clock. It was 3:33 a.m. Three sets of three. Suddenly, the thought of the time she had spent reading about angels came to the forefront of her mind. Rather than the panic or excitement one might feel at such a coincidence, Jane instead remembers feeling a warm, calming sensation come over her body. She took a few pictures of the time and the snow outside for the sake of posterity. And then, calmed by the thoughts she was having, drifted off to sleep once again.

By the time Jane stepped out of her house the next morning, the snow had melted. The strange events of the previous night had almost melted away too, and they were certainly not at the forefront of Jane's mind as she went about her business. During her lunch break, Jane was happy to receive a phone call from her husband. After a quick chat, she checked the phone to see how long they had spoken. It was one minute and eleven seconds. Another group of three. The numbers were beginning to be found everywhere. Once again, she put the thoughts to the back of her mind and went about her daily business.

Jane ran a blog. It was only a personal endeavor, but she liked the chance to share her thoughts with the world and would frequently write down a great deal. Once she shared these thoughts with the world, people would occasionally comment on her writing. Over the course of the coming days, she logged into the site of her blog to check whether there was any activity. She noticed that a new person had left a message on her blog. A person named Michael. Smiling at the coincidence, Jane felt a warm glow rising up inside of her. She was still encountering groups of three in her every day. They seemed to be everywhere. Jane responded to the message from Michael and thanked him for his influence.

Over the coming weeks, Jane felt the closeness of Michael rising up inside of her. Though there was never a dramatic moment when he might have revealed himself, Jane became more and more convinced that these constant occurrences were the sign she had asked for. To this day, whenever she begins to doubt to question an angel's influence in her life, Jane can immediately start to notice the signs appearing once again. She draws strength from this and finds it to be an entirely positive force for good in her life. For Jane, these signs of archangelic influence and power are more than enough of an indication that something beyond the obvious exists in our world.

Our next case comes from someone who has had a lifelong affinity with angels. This has not always been the case, however. As with many people, it took one moment of clarity to realize that the existence of archangels could be a force for good in a person's life. For our next entry, from a person named Joseph, being able to look back over twenty years brings a great deal of reflection and hindsight, allowing him to pinpoint one of the key moments in his life. Despite having been told about God and the existence of angels as a child, it was the events of one certain day that led him to believe in the relationship that he might possibly have with the archangels.

At the time, Joe was fifteen years old. As it is with many teenagers, this meant spending a lot of time asleep. During one particular morning, Joseph was still asleep. He woke suddenly and with a start. He had the feeling of a presence being nearby but was unable to detect exactly where it might be and could not see anyone else in the room. While this might have been alright had the spirit been a positive force, it felt very much as though there was a negative energy in the room. Unaware of exactly what was happening and still half asleep, Joseph could undoubtedly feel the evil force in his bedroom. He began to be gripped by panic.

As many people do in situations such as these, Joseph's mind began to travel back through his childhood. With the negative presence seemingly drawing closer and seemingly unable to move, he thought back to something his sister had told him when he was seven years old. She had mentioned that – should he ever feel the devil coming after him – he should place his trust in the Archangel Michael. By calling on the power of the angels, he might be able to draw the healing strength required to fight off even the world's most evil of forces.

Stuck in his bed, Joseph's thoughts travelled back to his sister's words. Though it was likely only a few seconds long, the next part of his life seemed to drag out for minutes and even hours. During this time, his sister's advice became clearer and clearer in his mind. With the negative energy drawing closer and closer, there was seemingly no other option. Shouting out into the darkness, Joseph called for help from the Archangels, asking for anyone to come down and help him. He asked to be saved.

Almost as soon as the words had left his lips, Joseph recalled a flash of blinding light filling the bedroom. In an instant, the fear and panic that was pinning him to the bed was gone. This was replaced with a new-found strength. A deafening sound filled his ears. It was almost as though an explosion had occurred right in the room. Just a second later, everything was back to normal. The room was quiet and calm. As Joseph opened up his eyes, he could see the room around him, and he could see himself lying flat on the bed. The negative presence had gone. From that day forward, it never returned.

While some might be quick to dismiss the encounter or to file it away as a ghost story or encounter with other paranormal beings, Joseph knew the truth. He had reached out to the archangels, and they had come to save him. For years, Joseph had struggled with his faith. Now, after that faithful night, he finally had enough information to make a decision. Whereas before he might have held archangels to be in the same category as Santa Claus or the Easter Bunny, they were now something truly powerful and truly worthy of his belief. His encounter with the evil spirit that crept into his room was not only enough to confirm his faith in God, but also enough to prompt a lifelong relationship with the archangels. From that point onwards, he knew of their power and felt happy enough to devote his whole life to them.

In the years since, Joseph has been able to hold their power incredibly close. In tough moments, he had been able to depend on the angels' healing powers and guidance to lead him through. Had he not experienced their power on that one night, he might never have welcomed their powers into his life. For this, he remains forever thankful. Having learned about the abilities of the archangels himself, Joseph now focuses on telling others about his stories and lets them know about how they might welcome similar experiences into their own lives.

The power of the archangels is not only something that can help us deal with minor worries and paranormal threats. The opportunity to depend upon and rely upon these powerful figures is often something that can be reassuring when we are facing some of the most trying and testing times in our lives. Not only are their powers useful in the moments themselves, but the healing qualities of the angelic forces can help us recover from and deal with all manner of testing things in our past. While it is always advisable that those suffering should seek out professional medical help, the ability to rely upon the reassuring qualities of religion and forces such as the archangels often helps people to recover.

During the next episode, we will witness how the power of archangels was able to help one young girl recover from a particularly traumatic experience. For those involved, the Divine power that reached out and touched the girl was a blessing. For those who were unsure of the healing powers beforehand, the chance to reflect upon the effect the angel's hand was truly extraordinary. In our story, the young girl is named Sally, but the events are recalled from the perspective of her mother, Alisa. The family lived in a nice home in Texas. The events took place around the end of 1993.

The story begins when Alisa came home one day to find that the home had been struck by burglars. The robbers had taken many of the more valuable possessions and trashed the home in the process. Their most disturbing crime had been to take hold of the young Sally, who happened to be home at the time, and make sure she didn't cry out for help. When Alisa arrived home to find that the house hand been ransacked, she discovered Sally tied up and left alone in the middle of the floor. While there was little in the way of lasting physical damage, Sally was notably shaken by the event. She struggled to remember what had happened and was struck by a case of amnesia. As well as this, she began to experience depressive episodes and seemed to be suffering from post-traumatic stress disorder. Coupled with her amnesia, her depression led to her having to relearn all of the ways she interacted with the world.

About a month after the burglary, Sally suffered a terrible seizure. Rushed to the hospital, doctors formalized the diagnosis of PTSD, announcing that Sally's seizures were causing terrible memories of the crime to flood back into her head. While she could not remember being attacked during her normal day, the sudden fits would involve these damaging memories to flash across Sally's mind's eye and cause real pain and damage.

Over time, some of the memories began to stay with Sally. She remembered how the burglars first entered the home, and when she first became suspicious of their presence. Not knowing how to react, she became hysterical. In an attempt to quiet the screaming girl, one of the robbers grabbed hold of her and tried to suffocate her using a pillow snatched from a bed. While he wrestled with the little girl, Sally noticed that he had a very specific tattoo. When the robber noticed that the girl has seen the distinguishing feature, he became enraged. In his fury, he struck her in the head. The force of the blow was enough to hurt the little girl and potentially led to the amnesia she was suffering.

In talking with her daughter about the experience afterwards, Alisa recollects exactly what her daughter said about brushing so close to death. Lying on the floor unconscious, unaware of how close she had come to dying, Sally instead entered into an almost dream-like state. Far from the burglary in her home, Sally found herself beneath a tree. Not sure of her surroundings, she remembers only that she experienced a feeling of utter bliss. The place beneath the tree felt warm and comforting. It was somewhere she wanted to spend the rest of her life. Alisa, when probing her daughter for more information, came to believe that the location was heaven or something like it. Sally then recalled a figure coming toward her. It was someone she knew, a man named Nicholas. Nicholas had died in the weeks leading up to the robbery. He sat down next to Sally and said that he had been sent by the archangels. He assured her that she was going to be alright. Without disclosing a reason why, he explained that she was to be spared. The next thing she knew, Sally was being introduced to the man who saved her. Rather than a physical description, she only recalls the bright, blinding light that she saw when looking toward the archangels. Once again, the feeling of warmth and healing comfort came over her. Speaking softly, he assured Sally that she would not only survive today, but that he would be watching over her for the rest of her life. In doing so, he was to be her guardian angel.

Finally, the angel dropped down next to Sally and whispered in her ear. Don't be afraid, he told her, she

42

would be returning back to her family soon. And then, put simply, she woke up. The circumstances she found herself in were, again, awful. She had been tied up and left alone in the house for her mother to find her. The violence of the situation would last with her for a long time. But as the memories of the attack came back, so did the memories of the angel. As Alisa began to learn about the burglary, she also saw the light in her daughter's life that came from her encounter with the angelic being. Sally began to receive psychological treatment from a therapist. Together, they helped piece together more and more information about the event, as well as helping Sally deal with the trauma of the terrible attack.

During one of these visits from her therapist, Sally was again struck by a traumatic episode. This time, rather than simply a fit, she seemed to become withdraw into herself. As the therapist watched on, Sally began rocking back and forth, her arms wrapped around her bended knees as she sat on the floor. No one seemed about to calm the young girl down. She seemed to be trying to sing, but the words would not come out properly. Her therapist rushed to help but struggled to calm the young girl down. She was no longer trying to listen to the outside world. Sally remembers that, as she was rocking back and forth, a bright light came into the room. Once again, her good friend stepped out from the light. Nicholas was there and came and sat down next to Sally. For the others in the room all of this was invisible. For Sally, it was incredibly real.

As she sat on the ground, rocking back and forth, both the therapist and Alisa seemed to give up. They couldn't get through to the child as she clutched at her knees. But unlike the fits, she did not seem to be in any kind of pain. Instead, there was a calm contentment on the little girl's face. Around the same time Nicholas appeared to her, the girl had stopped crying. Together, the pair talked through everything. Once again, Sally met up with her guardian angel. She gave him the pet name George, unable to pronounce the real name he told her. When she finally came back around into the room, Sally seemed happier than she had in weeks.

After that, Alisa noticed that the young child's healing process was greatly accelerated. With the angel known as George accompanying her, Sally seemed calmer. The anxiety attacks and traumatic episodes became less frequent. She knew that she had someone looking over her. Gradually, Alisa began to believe more and more in the story that her child was telling. After a short while, it became clear that this wasn't just a phase but was having a real, marked effect on Sally's recovery.

Visits from the angel who had come to be known as George had become more and more frequent. As Sally's healing process proceeded, Alisa would occasionally watch her daughter play. Sometimes, when the girl was laughing seemingly to herself, Alisa might ask what was funny. The child would always respond that George was making her laugh. As well as keeping the little girl entertained, he was helping her to recover from the horrific burglary attack. Rather than remaining afflicted by the violence, Sally was growing into a healthy young child, all with the help of her guardian angel. Alisa didn't know what to think.

One particularly memorable incident involved George's healing powers reaching out from the beyond the immediate vicinity of Sally's body. When a friend was struck down by a mystery illness and confined to her room, Sally snuck in. Once inside, she told her friend all about George and informed her friend that the angel would be helping with the healing process. Though unseen by the friend, George's influence seemed to work, and the friend began to get better.

As Sally grew older and as her traumatic past began to dissipate, her visits from George grew less and less frequent. However, Alisa recalls that whenever her daughter would fall sick or get injured, George would make a return. Unlike other children, Sally seemed to recover more quickly than anyone Alisa had even known. She always had the guardian angel watching over her. To this day, Alisa still believes in the healing powers of the archangels. While never having had to invoke the powers herself, she remains thankful for all of the help provided by George while her daughter was experiencing a terrible time.

Our next report comes from someone in the healing practice. This is an account from a doctor, it perhaps having a higher degree of credence for those who remain skeptical about the existence of archangels and their healing properties. In this passage, the doctor (who will be named Doctor Lamb) recalls the time when he encountered the healing powers of angels during his general practice. After coming across the phenomena, Dr Lamb's first instinct was to tell others. Though his accounts were disregarded by many of his colleagues, the stories found greater traction among the communities of people who work hard to preserve humanities knowledge of angels and their powers.

Just as in the case of the little girl who was traumatized by the burglary, many of the stories of angels that the doctor came across involved children who had near-death experiences. During these times of crisis, the guardian figures would appear to the children. While not all of the children who were close to death recounted similar experiences, it seemed as though almost half were able to tell a story about how an angel appeared to them and offered protection. For the most part, these were the children who recovered. As well as the angels' healing qualities, the doctor also remarked on the emotional support and hope that their appearance gave to the children. For those who were closest to death and in danger of losing hope, this sometimes made all of the difference.

Doctor Lamb's stories often involved his experiences learning under the guidance of an older colleague. While in his final months of training, he was transferred to one of America's top university hospitals. Without disclosing the name of the institution, it is safe to say that the hospital is widely known and associated with the very highest quality of medical care. At the time, Doctor Lamb was studying in the field of pediatrics. His teacher was a man with an almost encyclopedic knowledge of the body of science and medicine. There was very little that he had not seen during his tenure. As well as ensuring that all of his students were up to date with the most modern of medical journals, the teaching doctor also attempted to inject a slight touch of mysticism into all of his lessons. As a man who had once experienced his own near-death encounter, the redemptive and healing qualities of the angels were never far from his thoughts.

As might be expected of the medical community and trainee doctors, not every student took to these lessons. For his part, the teacher never tried to press this information on his students. Often, it was merely an interesting aside. But when a student took to the teachings – as Dr Lamb did – he soon formed a strong relationship with the student. One of the most common discussions between Dr Lamb and his mentor was the prospect of guardian angels and their roles in the near death experiences in children that the doctors encountered regularly.

Dr Lamb noted that his mentor was excited by all manner of teaching beyond the realm of what might be considered conventional medicine. Those children who died from diseases and illnesses just beyond the capabilities of modern science were the deaths that troubled Dr Lamb the most and the ones that he most sought to rectify. In doing so, he attempted to research the ideas of archangels and combine them with the hard science that he had spent his whole life learning. One particular case of a dying child had caused the teacher to stay up all night on one occasion. Despite his best efforts and the best medical care that money could buy, the child was still slipping away. Feeling increasingly powerless, Dr Lamb's mentor was facing increasingly sleepless nights. He felt utterly powerless. On this occasion, he finally fell asleep. In doing so, he was visited by a blinding white light. Just through the light, the doctor could make out the vague shape of a person. As well as the typical silhouette, the doctor was convinced that he could see the faint outline of wings. As he recounted to Dr Lamb, he felt like he nearly went blind from trying to look too far into the light. The being spoke to the doctor.

In many accounts of people who have been visited by angels, you will hear of a healing sense of warmth. Many of the stories we have recounted here involve a desire to heal a physical ailment. But for the doctor, it was a spiritual malady from which he suffered. Faced with the prospect of losing yet another small child in his care, the healing power of this angel brought with it reassurance. It spoke to him. As he explained to Dr Lamb, he had a full conversation with the archangel. During this time, the angel revealed the secret behind the deaths of these children that he could not save. The angel assured the doctor that, spiritually, he was a good man and that his efforts to save the children were appreciated by all. That some should have to pass as part of a greater plan was no fault of his own, and that the children themselves were often visited by angels and comforted in their final moments. For the doctor, this kind of reassurance was the drive that he needed to excel in his position.

And this was the important lesson that he tried to pass on to students. The healing qualities of the angel had made him into a better doctor. Because of the power of the archangels, he had become better at treated and caring for those children who came into his hospital. As Doctor Lamb recounts in his stories of guardian angels visiting the wards and helping children, it was perhaps the visit to his mentor that had the greatest effect of all. Not only did it imbue the man with the desire and the capability to become a better doctor, but it was knowledge that he passed on to those under his tutelage. If the saying goes that God works in mysterious ways, the appearance and help passed from the archangels to the teaching doctor just goes to show that their powers can also have a similarly widespread influence.

Our final story returns to the idea of an angelic vision. As one of the most common types of encounter that one might have with the Divine, these visions and visitations are often the moments that are referred to by believers when they are recounting the ways in which their belief in archangels has helped them. Often a defining moment in the life of the participant, the appearance of a guardian angel is a story that has been told many times. This story involves the accounts of a woman and her husband. For the purposes of this book, we will refer to them as Mary and Scott.

The story begins during the celebrations for Independence Day. As any American will know, the Fourth of July is often a day when everyone gets together to celebrate. It's almost universally a happy occasion, with fireworks, barbecues, family, and everyone having a good time. Despite the fact that Mary and Scott were not planning anything particularly special, they were still filled with the holiday spirit. Mary was working the next day and Scott was still recovering from a neck injury that had required surgery the previous month. Knowing that it was Scott's birthday the next weekend, they knew they would be able to delay their celebrations for just a few days more. However, they were thoroughly unprepared for what was going to happen.

On the morning of July 4th, Scott woke up in a terrible pain. Not only was he in agony, but he was having real trouble breathing. Noticing the issue right away, Mary grabbed the phone from the bedside table and called for an ambulance. Scott was a healthy, fit individual. The last thing that anyone had expected to happen would be a heart problem. Nevertheless, the doctors at the hospital quickly made their diagnosis and recommended a course of action. They got together with the husband and wife and told them that Scott would be needing heart bypass surgery right away.

Even before they could rush Scott to the theatre and begin the operation, another problem arose. The doctors had fitted a balloon pump to Scott's leg, attaching it to an artery and in doing so had cut off the circulation. A specialist was called in. The vascular surgeon took one look and was annoyed that he had not been summoned sooner. The problem was bad and if something was not done right away, there was the real chance that Scott might lose the leg. While her husband was still being treated, Mary was having trouble dealing with this.

Not knowing what to do, Mary reached out. Although she had been raised a Christian and was familiar with the word of God, she never would have regarded herself as a Christian. Despite this, in the moment of huge need, she reached out with a prayer. She didn't get down on her knees and hold her hands together. Instead, she simply held a deeply passionate thought in her mind. God, she asked, please return my husband to me.

As she thought the words to herself, Mary leaned back against the wall. She was in the waiting room while the doctors frittered around her husband and were trying to find the best course of treatment. As she leaned back, she could feel the coldness of the wall behind her. She closed her eyes. It was only for a second, but Mary was overcome by a strange sensation. It was almost like falling asleep. Indeed, at first she felt as though she was dreaming. Mary opened her eyes again, and she was back in the hospital waiting room. But something was different. This time there was a man she had not seen before. However, she could not see his face. He was sat on a seat facing away from Mary and looking towards the room where Scott was being treated.

Mary became intrigued. She tried to walk around the room to get a better look at the newcomer. Before she could reach the man and get a look at his face, she heard a voice that instructed her to sit down. Compelled, Mary did so. She sat in the seat behind the man, facing away from him. No one else in the room appeared to have heard anything. Instinctively, Mary knew not to turn around.

And, during one of the most difficult times in her life, Mary simply sat and talked to the man. During this moment, it felt as though time was standing still. As Mary talked, she could feel that the man's gaze never left the room where her husband was suffering. Mary talked about everything. For some reason, she felt compelled to talk and began to recall the story of how she and Scott met, how they had got married, and their entire life up to this point. As she told the story, Mary felt a warming glow come over her. Before she knew what had happened, she had reached the morning of the incident. After she had told the man what had happened that morning, he reassured her. The man informed Mary that her husband was under good care, that archangels were watching over him, and that she had nothing to fear. Finally, Mary turned around to see that the man had vanished. And with that, Mary woke up.

Mary found herself again in the hospital waiting room. Around her, everything seemed just as she left it. The man who had been listening to her talk was still missing. Looking around the room, it seemed as though no one was paying any attention to her, especially if she had just poured her heart out to the entire room. Just as she was waking up, a nurse ran into the waiting area. She scanned the room and her eyes fell on Mary.

The medical staff helped gather Mary into the room where Scott was recovering. While she had been away, the doctors had rushed him into surgery and operated.

Still groggy from the painkillers and anesthetic, Scott recalled to Mary that he had told the staff to just let her sleep. The hospital staff left Mary and Scott alone to talk things over.

Later, after the pair had returned from the hospital, a short while after celebrating Scott's birthday with a quiet party, they began to chat about what had happened on that day. Mary had never told anyone about the conversation she had held with the man in the hospital waiting room. However, when she began to confess what she had seen to Scott, they found that their stories matched up.

Scott could recollect that he had had an out-of-body experience. After agreeing to everything the doctors had suggested, he had been put under the effects of anesthesia. From here, he remembers rising up and out of his body. He was looking down at himself as he went under surgery. Far away in the distance, he could see Mary. She was not lying down, as he had expected, but was instead sat upright in a seat and talking animatedly. Scott could not hear what she was saying, but he remembers catching the eye of the man who was sitting beside her. When he did so, a great warming light came over him. The next thing he knew, he was being awakened by the doctors.

With their stories matching up, Mary has since developed a growing interest in the world of guardian archangels. Now a regular practitioner and a believer in the power of angel magick, she knows that she has someone watching over her and her husband.

Through the course of these stories, we have encountered many people who are on the brink of death. At that point, they are visited by divine beings named archangels. Thanks to the healing qualities of the angels, they are able to return to their normal lives. Not only are their bodies mended, but their spirits are stronger than ever before.

When it comes time to invoke your own archangels, you can look back on these stories as examples of what is possible when the going gets truly tough. Since this is a beginner's guide, we will first start with the essentials. Read on to the next chapter to learn more about the identities of the archangels.

Who are the archangels?

If you are to learn more about the archangels, then it can help to know exactly who they are. With the wealth of religious knowledge and tradition that has been passed down to us, it might seem easy enough to learn the names of the archangels and their relevant positions. However, the angelic pantheon is wide and varied. While many people find that their prayers are answered by Michael, Gabriel, or one of the other better-known angels, few people know that there is a specific guardian angel for every person. Before we begin the process of tracking down your guardian archangel, let's get to know the angels themselves.

Michael

For most people, Michael is the most important archangel. As we understand it, he was the first to be brought into this world by God and has taken on the mantle of the leader of the archangels. In this respect, his key qualities and areas of expertise are courage, strength, protection, integrity, and truth. Michael is known for the protection he provides to people, and the healing and guarding them emotionally, physically, and even psychically.

Many people have suggested that one of the key goals of Michael's existence is to rid the world of the toxins and particles most commonly associated with fear and panic. To accomplish this, he had a giant flaming sword. Many depictions of his form will include the sword as a point of reference. For those who suspect Michael might be nearby, flashes and bursts of light can be a good indicator that he is close. Should you feel yourself under psychic attack or when you are lacking in motivation, commitment, or dedication, Michael can be invoked. With his powers, people are able to realize their strength and overcome the difficulties in their lives.

Theologically, Michael is an interesting figure. It is said to be his sword that banished the fallen angel Satan, who was rebelling against God. It was Michael who was sent to the Garden of Eden, wherein he instructed Adam how to cultivate the land and make it his own. It was he who passed down many of the most important lessons to Moses. In 1950, he was added to the canon of Saints and became the patron saint of police officers and those who uphold the law. His powers are even useful when trying to heal things other than flesh and bone, with the modern issue of mechanical breakdown often being something people turn to Michael to solve.

For followers and believers, it is said that one of Michael's key qualities is the manner in which he helps people to follow their own personal truths without having to compromise. In doing this, we can discover our true natures and get to know ourselves better. If your job is feeling pressurized and you're finding it tough to meet deadlines, the support offered by the head of the archangels can be essential. As one of the most powerful figures in the archangel pantheon, Michael's powers can help in almost every situation.

Raphael

Like many of our writings about archangels, we can trace our knowledge of Raphael back to the ancient Hebrew Scriptures. Taken in the originally language, the word "raphe" means one who heals or a doctor, hinting at the power of the archangels who shares the name. Raphael is known as perhaps the most powerful healer among all of the angels. With his help, any type of healing is possible. Whether it is mental, physical, or spiritual, those who are in need of mending themselves should always turn towards his help. As well as personal healing, many people choose to trust Raphael when they want to heal other people. Without wanting to interfere in this other person's free will, it's possible to rely upon the help of the angel in order to help them from afar.

As well as his reputation as the best of the healers, many know Raphael as being one of the friendliest and even the funniest of all of the archangels. An often overlooked part of the angelic personality, his loving, kind, and humorous approach can be essential when trying to heal and mend people.

One of the best qualities offered by Raphael's work is his ability to release spirits and to heal spaces. Working hand in hand with Michael, he is adept at removing the negative influence that can be found in certain locations around the world. If you're feeling as though the negative energies of a particular place are hindering you, Raphael can be called upon to help remove them.

Another of Raphael's functions involves the protection of people on journeys. As the patron saint of people who are travelling, he has helped many people get through tough trips. To ensure safe passage, a quick prayer to Raphael can be very helpful. This can include everything along the way, from means of transportation to the accommodation you use. He can even help with lost luggage.

Known for his work with Tobias, many can recall the way in which Raphael taught Tobias how to create healing ointments and special balms in order to treat Tobias's father. Because of this, Raphael has since become the saint of surgeons and doctors. Added to the travelers, he has a great many people under his care and attention at any one time. For some people, Raphael's qualities as a healer go beyond this life. For anyone who believes that they have suffered greatly in a past life and that this may still be affecting them, a prayer to this archangel can be very helpful.

Gabriel

Gabriel is also one of the most famous archangels. Perhaps ranking alongside Michael in terms of fame, the name is familiar to many who have read texts from the Abrahamic religions. Unlike Raphael and Michael, Gabriel is frequently depicted as female. With the title of messenger, it's not uncommon for many artistic interpretations to focus both on Gabriel's role in the heavens and in her depiction as the highest ranking female archangel (at least, as far as gender applies to the angelic masses.) Along with Michael, she shares the honor of being one of only two angels mentioned directly by name during the Old Testament. As one of the most powerful archangels, those in need of strength and fortitude can call upon Gabriel when they are most in need.

As a messenger, Gabriel is renowned for delivering some of the most important details across the religious history of the world. It is she who tells Mary that she will soon give birth to a son who would grow up to become Jesus. She also went to Elizabeth, to tell her of the impending birth of her son, who would become John the Baptist. As such, many hopeful parents or those who are expecting a child find strength in calling on Gabriel.

If you ever feel that your spirituality is being hindered and that you are having trouble communicating with other planes, then Gabriel might be the one who is best placed to help. As God's messenger, she is the one who is most able to relay messages and clear the paths of communication. If you're finding it difficult to interpret dreams and visions, then she is also useful in this respect and can provide guidance.

Another of her roles is very useful to those who are involved in the artistic world or who are otherwise invested in communications. For these people, Gabriel can act as a kind of coach and can help with the refining and perfecting of messages and ideas. She can also help with the overcoming of procrastination and even fear.

With her special link with the word of God, Gabriel is the one who you need to invoke when hoping to discover your true calling. With her powers, she can provide guidance to humans and help them get on the right path. If you feel like you are straying from your intended path, then it is possible to call on her and hope to be set right once again. This might involve moving home, making a big purchase, or even moving into another career.

Like all archangels, Gabriel is essentially a healer. If you feel that toxins and negativity are beginning to take over your body, then her messages and words can bring a purifying touch to your life. As the only female archangel, she shares a special bond with other women and girls. As such, it is not uncommon for women to trust themselves unto Gabriel more readily than they might the other archangels.

Uriel

Of all of the archangels, it is perhaps Uriel who is considered the wisest. Due to the huge amount of knowledge that he has accumulated over the millennia, he had a great many insights into the world and can provide a huge number of practical solutions for those in need. At the same time, he is a very subtle being. Even without realizing that your prayers have been answered, Uriel may have been able to influence your life. This could arrive in the form of gradual change or a big eureka moment when you suddenly realize exactly what you have to do.

One of the most famous moments in the history of Uriel was when he warned Noah of the impending flood. Though not named directly in the Old Testament, we can surmise from other Scriptures that it was he who first told of the swathes of rain that would arrive. We also know that it was he who communicated ideas to Ezra, one of the prophets, including the prediction of the coming Messiah. His early communications with humanity helped form the basis of alchemy and many other early scientific endeavors.

Uriel is proficient in the art of divine magick. This makes him a favorite among magical practitioners and gives their actions a more sympathetic ear. Among the archangels, he is the one most likely to respond to the biggest of disasters, such as floods, earthquakes, and tsunamis. Not only can he heal an individual, but he can help with a society that needs to overcome trauma.

Uriel was once at the heart of a controversy in the early church. As the institutions became concerned about the zealous nature with which people were praising angels, they decided to remove a number of them from the pantheon. Uriel was among those culled. But this has not hindered him and archangel researchers today know him to be an essential member of the most powerful of all the angels.

Chamuel

An angel with many names, Chamuel is often considered to be a being of pure, clean love. As such, he is the ideal choice for those who are searching for help at times when they are depressed or in the very depths of their own sorrows. When trying to renew or repair relationships, he is the perfect choice. As something of a builder, he can work to build long-term bonds with others and help form connections between soul mates. When you are in need of a long lasting and rewarding relationship, then Chamuel is the archangel who is best placed to help.

As well as starting new relationships, we often encounter problems in keeping our existing relationships together. However, we can depend upon Chamuel to help repair and maintain even the most fractious bonds. These might be the relationships between a parent and a child, between brother and sister, or even romantic relationships. Should your relationship be cut short by death or separation, then Chamuel is the right choice for helping to overcome your problems.

Jophiel

As an angel present in the Garden of Eden, Jophiel has been involved with humanity right from the very start. As the overseer of beauty and art, there are few angels better placed to help you find the most gorgeous things in the world. To this extent, Jophiel has become the patron of artists and thinkers. His work helps us recognize and appreciate the wonders of the world in which we live. For those feeling their creative sparks dull, a quick prayer to Jophiel can be enough to get the artistic juices flowing once again. He provides energy and ability in equal measure, acting as an angelic muse when people seek to create something truly great. As well as seeing the beauty in art, he can help us see beauty in even the darkest and most twisted of people, helping us experience empathy.

A large part of being able to appreciate the beauty of the world around us is being able to slow down and not rush through life. If you feel you do not have enough time in the day to get everything done while still appreciating the world, then you may find a kindred spirit in Jophiel.

If you have the desire to awaken any kind of creative burning spirit within yourself, if you are feeling dormant and need to get going once again, then this is the archangel to suit your needs. Helping you better understand yourself and your desires, he can kindle the flame of artistic endeavor in the heart of any human. Often, his help arrives with us in the form of inspiration and bursts of ideas.

Raguel

The final archangel in the traditional pantheon of seven can often be the most overlooked. Raguel, however, fills an essential role in the world of the archangels. As the one in charge of fairness and justice in the world, he helps to watch over not only humanity, but also the other archangels. Under his guidance, they are better able to work as a team and as a group. With his help, they become the truly divine and helpful force that we have come to love. With the help of Raguel, the archangels are able to better help humanity and to better serve God.

But he is also the representative of the underrepresented. He is the archangel who represents the underdog. When you feel at a disadvantage or not as powerful as you might be, he is the one who can imbue you with a righteous energy and help you overcome even the most difficult of odds. He can help with communication, co-operation, and with finding harmony in the most discordant of situations. This is essential when resolving arguments or trying to get a team to work together.

Raguel takes on an important role at the end of the Bible. During the Revelation of John, the prophet foretells the end of the world. In this event, Raguel acts as the assistant to God, sounding the trumpet for the angels and leading them through the apocalypse. Come the end of the world, we might see Raguel's true power. Until then, his guiding hand leads the archangels in their healing missions.

Other Archangels

There are not only seven archangels. Though the ones we have covered are the key figures in many doctrines, there are also those angels that researchers have come to include in the panel. But who are they and what do you need to know about them?

Ariel

Also known as the Lion of God, Ariel has a long standing association with the big cats. Should he ever enter into your life, you might begin to see and notice more and more lions in the world around you, whether referenced in passing or actual physical representations. Heavily involved in the Judaism traditions, and especially Kabbalah, Ariel is known for his close work with King Solomon, as well as his ability to help people further their understanding of mysticism.

His position is focused on overseeing the water of the world. The spirits and animals associated with the seas and rivers on the planet come under his jurisdiction, including anything that lives or operates in the waters. Should you encounter an injured animal or a river in trouble, then it is Ariel who you need to invoke. He works closely alongside Raphael in order to make the most of the angels' healing powers.

Azrael

Azrael has a unique position in some religious traditions. Sometimes thought of as the Angel of Death, he is actually tasked with helping people cross over from our world into the world of heaven. At this point, he comforts and calms those who might be having trouble and ensures that suffering is always kept to a minimum. Once they have passed to the other side, Azrael can act as a guide and help the person get used to their new surroundings. Unlike the supposed fear many have of the idea of an Angel of Death, Azrael's position is nonetheless essential. His guiding hands help people through to the next world, and his role is vital for those travelling to the kingdom of heaven.

One common legend about Azrael involves his eyes. So closely linked with death, it is said that whenever he blinks, it represents the passing of another person. It is his job to oversee the world and to keep track of each birth and each death. As such, those who are struggling to come to terms with a death can look to Azrael for special assistance.

Camael

Camael is also known to some people as the angel who "sees God." As one of the most powerful archangels (though not one of the main seven,) he holds the honor of being able to stand in the presence of God on a regular basis. While some cultures have reimagined him as a God of War, a replacement for the Greek and Roman gods of old, he is simply another being in the angelic pantheon. Mostly relevant to Jewish mystical traditions, he is a figure who operates chiefly in heaven and spends comparatively little time on Earth when compared to the other archangels.

One of his most important roles is as a mediator, relaying the prayers he hears to God. For those who are struggling to be heard and are not feeling that their words are getting through, the chance to pray to Camael can help resolve this issue.

Haniel

Known to many angelic practitioners as the Grace of God, it is often thought that Haniel is one of the most principled and virtuous of the angels. When depicted in art or otherwise referred to, it is not uncommon to see him imagined as a prince or a duke. In the Jewish tradition, Haniel receives credit as the angel who guided Enoch through to the spiritual world and helped with his eventual ascension into the ranks of the angels.

Haniel's position among the angels is unique in that he is the person who people trust with the recovery of lost medical arts, such as potions or powders that have been lost to the ages. Those who pray to Haniel often hope to have this knowledge and ancient wisdom restored. As well as this, however, his aristocratic imaginings often mean that he is called upon to help those who are struggling with speaking in public. His charm and wit are essential for helping center these people and helping them overcome their fears.

Jeremiel/Ramiel

Operating under the names of Jeremial and Ramiel, these angels are in fact the same being. With a name taken to mean God's Mercy, this angel was a key figure in the writings of some of the most important early Jewish texts and feeds into our conceptions of the Old Testament God, as it is believed by all members of the Abrahamic religions.

Once we have crossed over from our current world into the next, it is Jeremiel who is charged with overseeing our life up until that point. This is not something that takes place once we die. Instead, he keeps an eye over the entire world while we are alive, in order to better review and adjust once we pass over. As such, anyone who is worried about the state of their immortal soul and wishes to make positive changes in their life might wish to pray to Jeremiel in order to be put along the right path as quickly as possible. In this respect, he is one of the key guiding archangels and can help to strengthen and equip us to better deal with the world around us.

Metatron

Metatron is a well-known but little understood member of the pantheon. Along with his brother Sandalphon, Metatron does not have a name ending in "el." He and Sandalphon are the only humans to ever have been transformed into archangels. As a human, he was known as Enoch. His story is told in the old religious texts. The origin of his name is still a mystery, but some have suggested that it reflects the true unspoken name of God, otherwise represented as Yahweh, and that he occupies a seat right next to the Lord himself.

For those in the western tradition, Metatron occupies a vital position. Each day, he receives word directly from God about which souls will be crossing over from one world into the next and delivers the orders to others to be carried out.

Before he became an angel, back when he was known as Enoch, Metatron worked chiefly as a scribe and wrote a great deal on the heavens. Considered by many to have been a prophet, his works included ideas and predictions about Noah, Adam, Solomon and even himself, as they were transmitted to him by the Angel Raziel. Once his good work was done, God asked the man to be escorted to the heavens, where he was turned into an angel. He was given his wings and told to continue his good work under the direct tutelage of God.

Similar to his position as a scribe while human, Metatron now keeps records of everything on Earth. His work – known as the book of life – is a record of everything that exists on the planet at all times. Thanks to this book, the relationship between the Earthly and the Divine is better understood. We can learn a great deal from the teachings and records we are lucky enough to receive from Metatron.

Metatron is known for his special bond with children. This became especially clear during the Exodus, when he helped to lead the children of Israel as they sought to venture through the wilderness. Leading them to safety back then, he is now able to help guide the children of the Earth and helps them as they journey through life.

Raziel

Working very closely with God himself, Raziel has a special insight into the secrets and the inner workings of the universe. Trusted with this information, he has even helped to pass on his teachings to humans such as Enoch. Once Adam and Eve were forced to leave the Garden of Eden, it was his teaching that helped them survive outside of paradise. He was also present to help Noah with both the building of the ark and with the rebuilding of the world after the great flood. Thanks to his knowledge of the universe, many people have benefitted from the teaching and understanding that he has passed down.

Because of this, he is the perfect archangel for those who are trying to comprehend abstract and esoteric teachings. As an angel who has communicated some of the most difficult ideas to humanity, he can be called upon when guidance and teaching is needed in daily life. With a quick prayer to this angel, you might be able to better study for a test or get a grip on a new job that is escaping your understanding. For those who are interested in the mystical arts, his guidance can better show you the way to practice magic.

Sandalphon

The brother of Enoch (later Metatron), Sandalphon was once a man known as Elijah. Like his twin brother, he was once a prophet and a person who formed a close personal bond with the Creator. As he ascended alongside his brother and turned into an archangel, he was also given an immortal assignment in order to act as a reward for all of his good work. He works from heaven and assists with the governance of the next life.

One of the most fascinating aspects of Elijah's transformation into Sandalphon was the method recorded in the Bible in the book 2 Kings. During his ascension, he was carried to heaven in a flaming chariot, dragged along at tremendous pace by a pair of horses made entirely of fire. Alongside him rode a whirlwind, carrying him up to the heavens.

These days, Sandalphon works chiefly with the prayers of humanity. He listens to everything and passes along the information to God. Said to be extremely tall, it is thought that he is tall enough that part of him may exist on two planes at once, representing his close bond with his former society. With his knowledge, he is the perfect angel for those who are looking for more information about the immediate future. In particular, expectant families have been known to ask him for help when curious about the gender of their soon-to-be-born child.

As ever with the worlds of the mystical, there are many things that we don't truly understand. To this point, the information we have just seen about the archangels represents the best of our knowledge about a world far, far different from our own. Of course, there are likely many more angels out there and many branches of mysticism that purport to know their names and character. As this is a beginner's guide, we have stuck to the basics and those we know to be true.

One of the key features of the guardian archangels is that each person on earth was born under the protective gaze of a particular angel. During the next chapter, we will begin to link you and your life with the protection of a divine being.

Finding your archangel

Now that we have an understanding of exactly who the angels are, it is important to know which one has that intrinsic link to your character. While all archangels can be invoked by anyone, and while their guidance and influence covers every human, each of us are born with a particular guardian angel. That makes our bond with that archangel extra strong and extra special. So how do we find out who our guardian angel is?

There are two main methods we use in this book. The first uses a system which many people are already familiar with. While less exact, it can give a good overview of the situation and is – in the majority of cases – correct. Should you feel that the result is slightly wrong, you may feel free to move on to the next step, which uses numerology to get an exact answer.

Using astrology

Though not traditionally an Abrahamic art form, astrology is very popular today. As such, it can be useful in giving us a good overview of the month in which we were born and how we are able to link the star cycles of our birth to the specific guardian ship of an archangel. Using the chart below, you can pair your birth with one of the archangels.

Let's look at the chart:

Cancer	Archangel Gabriel
Aries and Scorpio	Archangel Uriel
Gemini and Virgo	Archangel Chamuel
Sagittarius and Pisces	Archangel Jophiel
Taurus and Libra	Archangel Raziel
Capricorn and Aquarius	Archangel Jeremiel
Leo	Archangel Michael

This table makes everything simple. Once you know your astrological sign (based on the day you were born,) all you have to do is match this up against the relevant archangel. As such, those born under Leo will have Michael as a guardian angel. Those born under Aries or Scorpio will have Uriel as their guardian, and so on. While this chart is not perfect, it gives an excellent overview of the guardian angels and for most people returns an accurate result. If for any reason you do not feel satisfied with the result, then we can move on to the next step.

Using Numerology

Numerology is an ancient Kabbalistic tradition. Rising out of Jewish mysticism, it has been used over many millennia to find out many essential truths. Rather than delving too far into the history of the practice, we will only use the steps relevant to the finding of your guardian archangel.

First, you should write down your date of birth. Use only numbers and go from the smallest unit to the largest. So two digits representing days (01, 02… 10, 11 etc.), two digits representing months, and four digits representing a year. You will have one, long, eight-digit number.

Next, you will need to add each number to the one next to it. If, for example your date of birth was the first of July, 1970, the number would be 01071970. This would be added like 0+1+0+7+1+9+7+0 = 25.

Now, we need to reduce this to a single digit. If it is already, then great. If not, add the numbers together until you are left with one. So 25 would become 2+5, which would be 7.

Once you have your single digit, then you can look at this chart:

1	Archangel Gabriel
2 and 3	Archangel Uriel
4 and 5	Archangel Chamuel
6	Archangel Jophiel
7	Archangel Raziel
8	Archangel Jeremiel
9	Archangel Michael

Just as with the astrological method, all you need to do is pair your number with the relevant archangel and you will find the right guardian.

There are hundreds of other methods that are increasingly complex and are determined to use complicated formulas to match you with the right guardian angel. This can be found across the internet for those curious about the process.

During the next chapter, we will be focusing on more than just guardians. When learning how to invoke an archangel, we will be reaching out to many heavenly spirits. While it can be important to know exactly who is watching over you, those who take the lessons of this book to heart will realize that true power depends on being able to call upon the entire pantheon of archangels when in need.

How to invoke Archangels

During this chapter, we will look through some of the spells most often used to invoke the spirit and protection of the archangels. As well as depending on the protection of your guardian angel, you can turn to the pantheon of divine beings and bring them closer to your life. The spells come in various forms and are designed with different intentions.

Invocation for fulfilment

Calls on Michael, Raphael, Gabriel, and Uriel

Our first incantation is designed to help you achieve your goals. In order to do this, we will call on the powers of some of the most powerful archangels.

To get started, you will need a single white candle. Find an empty room, and turn off the lights. Clear a space on the floor, and place the candle in front of you. Light it.

While lighting the candle, whisper the four names of the angels, Michael, Raphael, Gabriel, and Uriel.

The next step is simple. Just remain seated and stare into the flame for four minutes. Breathe deeply during this time and keep the four names at the forefront of your mind.

Once four minutes have passed, lick the tips of your thumb and forefinger. Ensure you have a clear idea of the goal or objective you are hoping to realize. Say it aloud to the candle before pinching the flame out.

When the flame has been extinguished, close your eyes and say the angels' names one more time.

Let the smoke from the extinguished candle rise up into the room. Watch it rise. When it touches the ceiling, you can relight the candle, place it somewhere safe and allow it to burn down.

It is important never to tell anyone what you have wished for. Once the candle has burned down completely (this can be done in several stages), the spell will be complete. Start looking out for signs of the angels' influence in your life.

Prayer for Protection

Calls on: Michael

As the leader of the archangels, it should be no surprise to see that Michael is one of the most trusted by those who are calling for protection. With his sword and his leadership, he can help us banish even the most difficult of foes.

Because of this, it is common that people want to know how to invoke his presence and protection. What follows are two prayers designed to bring Michael closer to your life. A good time to use them is in the morning just after you rise from bed. They're simple incantations and can be used to bring protection into your entire day. Alternatively, they can be said before bed if you'd like to keep the negative emotions away while you sleep. The protection they bring lasts roughly fifteen hours.

The first invocation will depend on your visual powers.

When bringing Michael into your life, it can help to hold a picture of him in your head. While he might appear differently to most people, it is possible to look over the many artistic depictions of Michael in order to get a good starting point until your bond with the archangel is strengthened.

Once you have this image in your head, you will need to ensure you are thinking of him in the right context. Michael is the strongest of the archangels, the leader. When holding the image in your head, ensure that he is strong and powerful. It can help to picture the gleaming armor he might be wearing. Michael's flaming sword is one of his most noticeable features. Behind him, picture the hordes of angels who obey his every command. This is the powerful figure you need to hold in your mind's eye.

Whenever you encounter a negative emotion, experience, or sensation, bring the image to the front of your mind. For the briefest of seconds, picture Michael dealing with the problem. Picture him slaying your problems right in front of you. Try to notice the strength he employs. With this in mind, you can bring some of that very strength into your life.

As Michael's flaming sword slays the foes before him, you will become energized and know how to deal with the problem. While you will likely not have to slay anyone yourself, you can employ the same force of character when combatting your issues and bringing protective energy into your life.

The second invocation depends on your oratory abilities

If you are struggling with the visualization method, then it can help to rely on a quotation to bring forth the same feelings. As such, try repeating this passage when desiring protection in your life:

> *In the name of the Lord thy God, in His presence and benevolence, I call upon my own powers of self. I call upon strength and character. I call upon the force of the Archangel Michael, he who leads under the Creator. With his sword and his vision, he brings strength into my life. With his compassion and strength, he brings me comfort in hard times. In the name of the Lord and the presence of my own soul, I call upon and thank Michael for everything he can do, as permitted by the will of God.*

Saying this short incantation to yourself elicits the same emotion and feeling. When feeling weak or in need of protection, it can help to have it written down and carried about your person.

A protection for travelers

Calls on: Raphael

A journey can be stressful and worrying. These times are often when we're at our weakest and most in need of help. In circumstances such as these, Raphael is one of the most important archangels. Able to watch over travelers, his influence is ready to be called upon. One of the best ways is using this simple incantation. Unlike the others, it is slightly longer.

The invocation can be repeated at any time during the trip, allowing the traveler to call upon Raphael during the journey.

Lord, send Raphael to help me on my way,

Lord, send Raphael to help me reach my goal,

Lord, send Raphael to help me on my way,

Lord, send Raphael to help me towards home,

Lord, above, Lord, below,

Lord, send Raphael to help me on my way,

The protecting love holds me

The protecting love shields me

The protecting love guides me

As I journey forth.

Once you have memorized the passage, then it can be repeated to yourself as often as you like. Whether you're driving or sitting on a train, start to look out for the slight indications that an angelic presence might be nearby.

An invocation for achieving goals

Calls on: Gabriel, Uriel, and Raphael

Often, one of our chief goals with calling on the power of the angels is in helping us to reach goals and objectives. When we want something but feel we're not yet ready for it, then the healing powers of angels can help us make that extra step.

To accomplish this spell, it is best to have an empty room at a time close to midnight. Again, we will need a single candle of any color. Place the candle in front of you and sit cross legged. Write down your objective or goal on a piece of paper and place it at the base of the candle. Then, light the wick. Sit for five minutes and consider the words written on the paper. Stare into the candle's flame and say the names of the three angels over and over while doing so. Unlike the earlier spell, we will not extinguish this candle. Instead, use the flame to lightly sear the edges of the paper, just enough that a little smoke rises. Do not burn the paper. Once the edges are charred, then place the paper at the base of the candle and allow it to burn until it is no more. During this time, you are free to leave the candle's presence. Before you do so, thank the angels each in turn and make the sign of the cross over your body.

As the candle burns out, the words written on the paper should resonate around the room. Soon, if done correctly, the angelic magick will begin to influence your life.

A call to dreams

Calls on: Michael

Dreams play a big part in our interaction with archangels. Often, people report that they communicated with divine beings while unconscious. As such, being able to break down the barriers between our world and theirs can rely on dreams to make this happen. Our final invocation focuses on exactly that.

In this invocation, we will call on the most powerful of all archangels. Michael and his flaming sword are exactly the kind of thing dreams are made of, and his strong presence is sure to leave a mark on even the deepest of sleepers.

Traditionally, this process was carried out with an oil lamp. These days, a candle placed inside a lantern can have the same effect. These items can be purchased from many department stores. Furthermore, a pinch of salt is required. When you have everything ready, you can begin.

It can help to carry out this process late at night, when you have just had a shower. When you are feeling slightly tired and have cleansed yourself, then you will be in a more receptive state.

First light your lamp or candle. Hold the pinch of salt near the light and let it sprinkle on the floor. This will purify the area around you.

Next, you will need to whisper into the source of the light. Repeat the below incantation for ten minutes.

Light this lamp to reach out to Michael

Light this lamp, should my words be true

Show me the water and the grave beyond

Show me the world you have built out of stone.

Now, to sleep, to see the Lord's work.

Repeat this phrase for ten minutes. Stare into the light as you do so. You should feel yourself lulling into a sleepy state. Once complete, allow the light to remain lit through the night. It will stand vigil over you as you sleep.

Go to bed and lay your head on the pillow. Allow yourself to be overcome by sleep. If the words were said correctly and your faith is true, the ideas and symbols of angels should filter into your dreams. As they do so, the power of the archangels will enter steadily into your life.

Conclusion

As you have seen in this guide, there are many ways in which the archangels are able to influence our lives. As you become more and more acquainted with their power, you may realize the extent to which they hold sway over our existence. If you are interested in learning more, there is a reading list at the end of this book.

For those who are getting to grips with the advice and teachings included at the end of this book, perhaps the best instruction is to simply keep practicing and to never give up faith. When calling upon divine beings such as archangels, it can often be the supreme amount of faith you have in the process that is able to make the invocation work.

Once you have mastered your faith and mastered the power of the angels, there will be little else holding you back from a truly happy existence. Good luck!

Further reading

Abdel Haleem, M. (2008). *The Qur'an*. Oxford: Oxford University Press.

Carroll, R. and Prickett, S. (2008). *The Bible*. Oxford: Oxford University Press.

Cooper, D. and Whild, T. (n.d.). *Archangel guide to ascension.*

Core, C. (2012). *Angelic Reiki*. Bloomington, IN: Balboa Press.

Grant, R. (2005). *Edgar Cayce on angels*. Virginia Beach, Va.: A.R.E. Press.

Jewish Publication Society, (1992). *The Torah*. Philadelphia, PA: Jewish Publication Society.

Mackenzie, R. (2013). *Metatron*. Lexington, KY: Amazon.

Prophet, E. (2008). *I am your guard*. Gardiner, MT: Summit University Press.

Steiner, R. and Bamford, C. (1994). *The Archangel Michael*. Hudson, N.Y.: Anthroposophic Press.

Virtue, D. (2003). *Archangels & ascended masters.* Carlsbad, Calif.: Hay House.

Virtue, D. (2009). *The miracles of Archangel Michael.* London: Hay House.

Virtue, D. (2010). *The healing miracles of Archangel Raphael.* Carlsbad, Calif.: Hay House, Inc.

Virtue, D. (2011). *Archangels 101.* London: Hay House.

Virtue, D. (n.d.). *The Miracles of Archangel Gabriel.*

About the Author

Conrad Bauer is passionate about everything paranormal, mysterious, and terrifying. It comes from his childhood and the famous stories his grandfather used to tell the family during summer vacation camping trips. He vividly remembers his grandfather sitting around the fire with new stories to tell everyone who would gather around and listen. His favorites were about the paranormal, including ghost stories, haunted houses, strange places, and paranormal occurrences.

Bauer is an adventurous traveller who has gone to many places in search of the unexplained and paranormal. He has been researching the paranormal and what scares people for more than four decades. He has accumulated a solid expertise and knowledge that he now shares through his books with his readers and followers.

Conrad, now retired, lives in the countryside in Ireland with his wife and two dogs.

Just click on the cover to check them out.

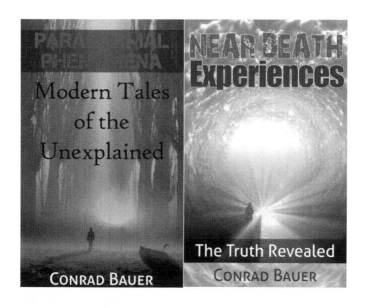

Made in the USA
Lexington, KY
02 August 2016